AN ORDINARY WOMAN

an ordinary
woman

by LUCILLE CLIFTON

 RANDOM HOUSE, NEW YORK

Library of Congress Cataloging in Publication Data

Clifton, Lucille, 1936-
An ordinary woman.
Poems.
I. Title.
PS3553.L4507 811'.5'4 74-9080
ISBN 0-394-49468-7
ISBN 0-394-70942-X (pbk.)

Manufactured in the United States of America
9 8 7 6 5 4 3 2

First Edition

to Fred
you know you know me well

Contents

sisters

i agree with the leaves

❦ ❦ sisters

In Salem

TO JEANETTE

Weird sister
the Black witches know that
the terror is not in the moon
choreographing the dance of wereladies
and the terror is not in the broom
swinging around to the hum of cat music
nor the wild clock face grinning from the wall,
the terror is in the plain pink
at the window
and the hedges moral as fire
and the plain face of the white woman watching us
as she beats her ordinary bread.

4

Sisters

FOR ELAINE PHILIP ON HER BIRTHDAY

me and you be sisters.
we be the same.
me and you
coming from the same place.
me and you
be greasing our legs
touching up our edges.
me and you
be scared of rats
be stepping on roaches.
me and you
come running high down purdy street one time
and mama laugh and shake her head at
me and you.
me and you
got babies
got thirty-five
got black
let our hair go back
be loving ourselves
be loving ourselves
be sisters.
only where you sing
i poet.

❦ 6

Leanna's Poem

FOR LEANNA WEBSTER

one
is never enough for me
you said
surrounded by the lunch
we could not taste for eating,
and i smiled and thought about meals
and mealmates and hunger
and days and time and life and
hunger, and you are right
it is not, it is never enough;
and so this poem is for us,
Leanna, two hungry ladies,
and i wish for you
what i wish for myself—
more than one
more than one
more than one.

🌷 8

On the Birth of Bomani

FOR JARIBU AND SABABU

we have taken the best leaves
and the best roots
and your mama whose skin
is the color of the sun
has opened into a fire and
your daddy whose skin
is the color of the night
has tended it carefully with
his hunter's hands and
here you have come, Bomani,
an Afrikan Treasure-Man.
may the art in the love that made you
fill your fingers,
may the love in the art that made you
fill your heart.

10

Salt

FOR SJ AND JJ

he is as salt
to her,
a strange sweet
a peculiar money
precious and valuable
only to her tribe,
and she is salt
to him,
something that rubs raw
that leaves a tearful taste
but what he will
strain the ocean for and
what he needs.

12

A Storm Poem

FOR ADRIENNE

The wind is eating
the world again.
Continents spin
on its vigorous tongue
and you Adrienne
broken like a bone
should not sink
casual as dinner.
Adrienne.
I pronounce your name.
I push your person
into the throat
of this glutton.
For you
let the windmouth burn at last.
For you
let the windteeth break.

God's Mood

these daughters are bone,
they break.
He wanted stone girls
and boys with branches for arms
that He could lift His life with
and be lifted by.
these sons are bone.

He is tired of years that keep turning into age
and flesh that keeps widening.
He is tired of waiting for His teeth to
bite Him and walk away.

He is tired of bone,
it breaks.
He is tired of eve's fancy and
adam's whining ways.

New Bones

we will wear
new bones again.
we will leave
these rainy days,
break out through
another mouth
into sun and honey time.
worlds buzz over us like bees,
we be splendid in new bones.
other people think they know
how long life is
how strong life is.
we know.

❦ 18

Harriet
if i be you
let me not forget
to be the pistol
pointed
to be the madwoman
at the rivers edge
warning
be free or die
and Isabell
if i be you
let me in my
sojourning
not forget
to ask my brothers
ain't i a woman too
and
Grandmother
if i be you
let me not forget to
work hard
trust the Gods
love my children and
wait.

20

Roots

call it our craziness even,
call it anything.
it is the life thing in us
that will not let us die.
even in death's hand
we fold the fingers up
and call them greens and
grow on them,
we hum them and make music.
call it our wildness then,
we are lost from the field
of flowers, we become
a field of flowers.
call it our craziness
our wildness
call it our roots,
it is the light in us
it is the light of us
it is the light, call it
whatever you have to,
call it anything.

❧ 22

Come home from the movies,
Black girls and boys,
the picture be over and the screen
be cold as our neighborhood.
Come home from the show,
don't be the show.
Take off some flowers and plant them,
pick us some papers and read them,
stop making some babies and raise them.
Come home from the movies
Black girls and boys,
show our fathers how to walk like men,
they already know how to dance.

To Ms. Ann

i will have to forget
your face
when you watched me breaking
in the fields,
missing my children.

i will have to forget
your face
when you watched me carry
your husband's
stagnant water.

i will have to forget
your face
when you handed me
your house
to make a home,

and you never called me sister
then, you never called me sister
and it has only been forever and
i will have to forget your face.

My Boys

FOR CHAN AND BAGGY

My boys beauty is
numberless. No kit
can find their colors
in it. Only Afrikan artists,
studying forever, can
represent them. They are
brothers to each other
and to other live and
lovely things. People
approaching my boys
in their beauty
stand stunned
questioning over and over—
What is the meaning of this?

28

Last Note to My Girls

FOR SID, RICA, GILLY AND NEEN

my girls
my girls
my almost me
mellowed in a brown bag
held tight and straining
at the top
like a good lunch
until the bag turned weak and wet
and burst in our honeymoon rooms.
we wiped the mess and
dressed you in our name and
here you are
my girls
my girls
forty quick fingers
reaching for the door.

i command you to be
good runners
to go with grace
go well in the dark and
make for high ground
my dearest girls
my girls
my more than me.

A Visit to Gettysburg

i will
touch stone
yes i will
teach white rock to answer
yes i will
walk in the wake
of the battle sir
while the hills
and the trees
and the guns watch me
a touchstone
and i will rub
"where is my black blood
and black bone?"
and the grounds
and the graves
will throw off they clothes
and touch stone
for this touchstone.

32

Monticello

(History—Sally Hemmings, slave at Monticello, bore several children with bright red hair)

God declares no Independence.
Here come sons
from this Black Sally
branded with Jefferson hair.

❦ 34

To a Dark Moses

you are the one
i am lit for.
come with your rod
that twists
and is a serpent.
i am the bush.
i am burning.
i am not consumed.

Kali
queen of fatality, she
determines the destiny
of things. nemesis.
the permanent guest
within ourselves.
woman of warfare,
of the chase, bitch
of blood sacrifice and death.
dread mother. the mystery
ever present in us and
outside us. the
terrible Hindu Woman God
Kali.
who is Black.

this morning

(FOR THE GIRLS OF EASTERN HIGH
SCHOOL)

this morning
this morning
      i met myself
coming in

a bright
jungle girl
shining
quick as a snake
a tall
tree girl a
me girl
      i met myself
this morning
coming in

and all day
i have been
a black bell
ringing
i survive
      survive
survive

❧ ❧ i agree with the leaves

The Lesson of the Falling Leaves

the leaves believe
such letting go is love
such love is faith
such faith is grace
such grace is god
i agree with the leaves

❦ 44

i am running into a new year
and the old years blow back
like a wind
that i catch in my hair
like strong fingers like
all my old promises and
it will be hard to let go
of what i said to myself
about myself
when i was sixteen and
twentysix and thirtysix
even thirtysix but
i am running into a new year
and i beg what i love and
i leave to forgive me

❦   46

The Coming of Kali

it is the Black God, Kali,
a woman God and terrible
with her skulls and breasts.
i am one side of your skin,
she sings, softness is the other,
you know you know me well, she sings,
you know you know me well.

running Kali off is hard.
she is persistent with her
Black terrible self. she
knows places in my bones
i never sing about but
she knows i know them well.
she knows.
she knows.

❦ 48

She Insists On Me

i offer my
little sister up. no,
she says, no i want
you fat poet with
dead teeth. she insists
on me. my daughters
promise things, they
pretend to be me but
nothing fools her
nothing moves her and
i end up pleading
woman woman i am trying
to make a living here,
woman woman you are not
welcome in these bones,
woman woman please but she
walks past words and
insists on me.

50

She Understands Me

it is all blood and breaking,
blood and breaking. the thing
drops out of its box squalling
into the light. they are both squalling,
animal and cage. her bars lie wet, open
and empty and she has made herself again
out of flesh out of dictionaries,
she is always emptying and it is all
the same wound the same blood the same breaking.

❦ 52

She Is Dreaming

sometimes
the whole world of women
seems a landscape of
red blood and things
that need healing,
the fears all
fears of the flesh;
will it open
or close
will it scar or
keep bleeding
will it live
will it live
will it live and
will he murder it or
marry it.

Her Love Poem

Demon, Demon, you have dumped me
in the middle of my imagination
and i am dizzy with spinning from
nothing to nothing. It is all your fault
poet, fat man, lover of weak women
and i intend to blame you for it.
I will have you in my head
anyway i can, and it may be love you
or hate you but i will have you
have you have you.

❦ 56

Calming Kali

be quiet awful woman,
lonely as hell,
and i will comfort you
when i can
and give you my bones
and my blood to feed on.
gently gently now
awful woman,
i know i am your sister.

❦ 58

I Am Not Done Yet

as possible as yeast
as imminent as bread
a collection of safe habits
a collection of cares
less certain than i seem
more certain than i was
a changed changer
i continue to continue
where i have been
most of my lives is
where i'm going

🌷 60

The Poet

i beg my bones to be good but
they keep clicking music and
i spin in the center of myself
a foolish frightful woman
moving my skin against the wind and
tap dancing for my life.

Turning

turning into my own
turning on in
to my own self
at last
turning out of the
white cage, turning out of the
lady cage
turning at last
on a stem like a black fruit
in my own season
at last

❦   64

My Poem

a love person
from love people
out of the Afrikan sun
under the sign of Cancer.
whoever see my
midnight smile
seeing star apple and
mango from home.
whoever take me for
a negative thing,
his death be on him
like a skin
and his skin
be his heart's revenge.

❧ 66

lucy one-eye
she got her mama's ways.
big round roller
can't cook
can't clean
if that's what you want
you got it world.

lucy one-eye
she see the world sideways.
word foolish
she say what she don't want
to say, she don't say
what she want to.

lucy one-eye
she won't walk away
from it.
she'll keep on trying
with her crooked look
and her wrinkled ways,
the darling girl.

❦ 68

if mama
could see
she would see
lucy sprawling
limbs of lucy
decorating the
backs of chairs
lucy hair
holding the mirrors up
that reflect odd
aspects of lucy.

if mama
could hear
she would hear
lucysong rolled in the
corners like lint
exotic webs of lucysighs
long lucy spiders explaining
to obscure gods.

if mama
could talk
she would talk
good girl
good girl
good girl
clean up your room.

i was born in a hotel,
a maskmaker.
my bones were knit by
a perilous knife.
my skin turned round
at midnight and
i entered the earth in
a woman jar.
i learned the world all
wormside up
and this is my yes
my strong fingers;
i was born in a bed of
good lessons
and it has made me
wise.

light
on my mother's tongue
breaks through her soft
extravagant hip
into life.
Lucille
she calls the light,
which was the name
of the grandmother
who waited by the crossroads
in Virginia
and shot the whiteman off his horse,
killing the killer of sons.
light breaks from her life
to her lives . . .

mine already is
an Afrikan name.

Cutting Greens

curling them around
i hold their bodies in obscene embrace
thinking of everything but kinship.
collards and kale
strain against each strange other
away from my kissmaking hand and
the iron bedpot.
the pot is black,
the cutting board is black,
my hand,
and just for a minute
the greens roll black under the knife,
and the kitchen twists dark on its spine
and i taste in my natural appetite
the bond of live things everywhere.

Jackie Robinson

ran against walls
without breaking.
in night games
was not foul
but, brave as a hit
over whitestone fences,
entered the conquering dark.

i went to the valley
but i didn't go to stay

i stand on my father's ground
not breaking.
it holds me up
like a hand my father pushes.
Virginia.
i am in Virginia,
the magic word
rocked in my father's box
like heaven,
the magic line in my hand. but
where is the Afrika in this?

except, the grass is green,
is greener he would say.
and the sky opens a better blue
and in the historical museum
where the slaves
are still hidden away like knives
i find a paper with a name i know.
his name.
their name.
Sayles.
the name he loved.

i stand on my father's ground
not breaking.
there is an Afrikan in this
and whose ever name it has been,
the blood is mine.

my soul got happy
and i stayed all day.

❦ 80

at last we killed the roaches.
mama and me. she sprayed,
i swept the ceiling and they fell
dying onto our shoulders, in our hair
covering us with red. the tribe was broken,
the cooking pots were ours again
and we were glad, such cleanliness was grace
when i was twelve. only for a few nights,
and then not much, my dreams were blood
my hands were blades and it was murder murder
all over the place.

In the Evenings

i go through my rooms
like a witch watchman
mad as my mother was for
rattling knobs and
tapping glass. ah, lady,
i can see you now,
our personal nurse,
placing the iron
wrapped in rags
near our cold toes.
you are thawed places and
safe walls to me as i walk
the same sentry,
ironing the winters warm and
shaking locks in the night
like a ghost.

Breaklight

light keeps on breaking.
i keep knowing
the language of other nations.
i keep hearing
tree talk
water words
and i keep knowing what they mean.
and light just keeps on breaking.
last night
the fears of my mother came
knocking and when i
opened the door
they tried to explain themselves
and i understood
everything they said.

some dreams hang in the air
like smoke. some dreams
get all in your clothes and
be wearing them more than you do and
you be half the time trying to
hold them and half the time
trying to wave them away.
their smell be all over you and
they get to your eyes and
you cry. the fire be gone
and the wood but some dreams
hang in the air like smoke
touching everything.

❦ 88

the carver

FOR FRED

sees the man
in the wood and
calls his name and
the man in the wood
breaks through the bark and
the nations of wood call
the carver
Brother

❦ 90

let there be new flowering
in the fields let the fields
turn mellow for the men
let the men keep tender
through the time let the time
be wrested from the war
let the war be won
let love be
at the end

the thirty eighth year
of my life,
plain as bread
round as a cake
an ordinary woman.

an ordinary woman.

i had expected to be
smaller than this,
more beautiful,
wiser in Afrikan ways,
more confident,
i had expected
more than this.

i will be forty soon.
my mother once was forty.

my mother died at forty four,
a woman of sad countenance
leaving behind a girl
awkward as a stork.
my mother was thick,
her hair was a jungle and
she was very wise
and beautiful
and sad.

i have dreamed dreams
for you mama
more than once.
i have wrapped me
in your skin
and made you live again

more than once.
i have taken the bones you hardened
and built daughters
and they blossom and promise fruit
like Afrikan trees.
i am a woman now.
an ordinary woman.

in the thirty eighth
year of my life,
surrounded by life,
a perfect picture of
blackness blessed,
i had not expected this
loneliness.

if it is western,
if it is the final
Europe in my mind,
if in the middle of my life
i am turning the final turn
into the shining dark
let me come to it whole
and holy
not afraid
not lonely
out of my mother's life
into my own.
into my own.

i had expected more than this.
i had not expected to be
an ordinary woman.

LUCILLE CLIFTON was born in Depew, New York, in 1936, and attended Howard University and Fredonia State Teachers College. She now lives in Baltimore with her husband and their six children. Mrs. Clifton's previous collections of poetry are *Good Times* and *Good News About the Earth*. She has also written three children's books: *Some of the Days of Everett Anderson*, *The Black BC's*, and *Everett Anderson's Christmas Coming*. Her work has appeared in *Ms.*, *Black World*, *The Massachusetts Review*, and various other places. She participated in the YW–YMHA Poetry Center's Discovery Series for 1961, and has given readings in many colleges and universities.